Exercises

AT THE

ORDINATION

OF

FIVE MISSIONARIES,

UNDER APPOINTMENT OF THE
AMERICAN BOARD.

Chicago, April 18th, 1867.

CHICAGO:
AMERICAN BOARD OF COMMISSIONERS FOR FOREIGN MISSIONS,
PUBLISHED BY THE DISTRICT SECRETARY.
1867.

ORDINATION OF MISSIONARIES.

In response to Letters Missive issued by the Union Park Congregational Church of Chicago, a council convened April 15th, 1867, to examine, and ordain, if approved, the following persons as Foreign Missionaries: William E. DeRiemer, Samuel E. Evans, Carmi C. Thayer, Spencer R. Wells, and William Henry Atkinson.

These young men were members of the graduating class of Chicago Theological Seminary.

The churches invited to sit in the council, were the Congregational and N. S. Presbyterian Churches of Chicago, Plymouth Congregational Church, Milwaukee, the Congregational Churches of Appleton, Paris and Bristol, Berlin and Delavan, Wisconsin; Farmington, Normal, Harvard, Lisle and Jacksonville, Illinois; Dana, Massachusetts; Berkley St. Church, Boston; and the Broadway Church, Chelsea, Massachusetts. The following ministers were also invited: Rev. T. M. Post, D.D., St. Louis, Rev. Prof. Henry Smith, D.D., Lane Seminary, Rev. G. W. Wood, D.D., Secretary A.B. C. F. M., New York, Rev. Profs. J. Haven, D.D., S. C. Bartlett, D.D., and F. W. Fisk, D.D., Revs. H. L. Hammond, G. S. F. Savage, J. E. Roy, and S. J. Humphrey.

The council was organized by choosing Rev. Wm. W. Patton, D.D., Moderator, and Rev. S. J. Humphrey, Scribe.

After a peculiarly interesting relation of their christian experience, by the candidates, and of the motives which had led them to desire the ministry and the missionary work, they were examined in their views of christian doctrine. The council then voted unanimously to proceed to set them apart for the work to which they had been manifestly called.

The ordination took place at the Second Presbyterian Church of Chicago, April 18th. A crowded audience were in attendance, and the services were of the most interesting and impressive character.

SERMON.

The Sermon was preached by Prof. HENRY SMITH, D.D., Lane Seminary, Walnut Hills, Ohio, from the text — "And I, if I be lifted up, will draw all men unto me. (John xii. 32.) The limits of this pamphlet allow only the closing portion of it to be given. It was an able and eloquent presentation of the *Attraction of the Cross*, by indicating *some of the universal and controlling principles of human action, to which the great truths represented in the tragedy of Calvary make their appeal.* The conclusion was in the following words:

In the full faith of the power of this blessed Gospel to subdue the world to Christ, Lane sends, through me, her best greetings, her joyful gratulations, her heartiest "All hail" to her sister Seminary of Chicago. Not with envy, but with joy does she behold her sister in one noble gift, reaching one-fourth the entire number, which, during a motherhood of five and thirty years, she herself has been able to consecrate to the work of Foreign Missions. Yet with tears of thanksgiving, she points to her own twenty sons, who have listened to the Macedonian cry of the world of heathen darkness. Some of them, indeed, have fallen asleep in Jesus, but most of them continue to this present.

The beloved young brethren who are to receive our "God speed you" to-night, Lane charges with a commission of love to her own well-remembered sons. To whatever section of the globe, shrouded in heathen darkness, you bend your steps, you will find them there. Bear, then, the salutations—yea, the heartfelt love and benedictions of their theological mother to the Williamsons, father and son, among the red men of the West; to Bushnell and Preston, in Africa; to Smith and Montgomery, in Turkey; to Shedd, in Persia; to Chandler and White, in India; to Williams and Stanley, in China; to Andrews and Pogue, in the islands of the sea; — and especially does she charge you not to pass by without a visit to the sacred mounds which mark the last resting-place of her departed and glorified children. She charges you to drop a tear, and, if Providence permits it, to plant some green and fragrant shrub, in token of her unforgetting love, at the graves of Caswell and Spaulding, and Campbell and Bonney—of Cummings, and Wheeler, and Porter.

Men and brethren, ministers, messengers and members of Christ's churches in the West, whom this unwonted spectacle has drawn together to-night, are you ready for this sacrifice? I know that you are ready, for this act is full of the very spirit of Christ. This good news is for all men. You believe that. It is suited to the nature and to the condition of all men. You believe that. It is to be published in the ears of all men. You believe that. But when, O Christian—when? Gird yourself, I beseech you, in whatever vocation Christ has called you to labor—gird yourself anew and instantly for this work. Christ has laid it upon you; Christ has laid it upon me. Go ye into all the world, and preach the Gospel to every creature. Go in person—go by proxy—go now, for now is the time in which men are perishing for the lack of this Gospel. God has laid this work upon *us*, in whatever form of effort he has called us to serve him.

Let us labor for it—let us pray for it—let us give for it; and as we labor, pray and give, let us have faith in the principles and in the power of the Gospel. It shall triumph—Christ hath promised it: "And I, if I be lifted up from the earth, will draw all men unto me." God hath declared it: "To him every knee shall bow and every tongue confess." It shall prevail, and spread, and prosper, until the kingdom, and the greatness of the kingdom, under the whole heaven, shall be given to the people of the saints of the Most High God. Oh, wonderful scheme of redemption! Oh, love infinite and unsearchable! What heart will not respond to it? What Christian will not rejoice in it? What poor, perishing sinner will not be melted by it into penitence and love?

"Oh, the sweet wonders of that Cross,
Where my Redeemer loved and died!
Her noblest life my spirit draws
From his dear wounds and bleeding side.

"I would for ever speak his name
In sounds to mortal ears unknown;
With angels join to praise the Lamb,
And worship at his Father's throne."

Rev. Truman M. Post, D.D., St. Louis, offered the ordaining prayer, assisted by the following ministers in the laying on of hands: Rev. R. W. Patterson, D.D., Rev. S. B. Treat, Prof. J. Haven, D.D., Rev. P. C. Pettibone, Rev. Z. M. Humphrey, D.D., Rev. C. D. Helmer, Prof. S. C. Bartlett, D.D., Rev. J. Collie, President J. M. Sturtevant, D.D., and Rev. L. Taylor.

CHARGE.

PROF. SAMUEL C. BARTLETT, CHICAGO THEOLOGICAL SEMINARY.

My Dear Young Brethren, — History repeats itself to-night. Fifty-five years ago, in the oldest city of New England, Judson, and Newell, and Mills, and Nott, and Rice, stood up before Spring, and Morse, and Worcester, and Woods, and Griffin, for missionary ordination—the first fruits of America and of Andover. Instead of the fathers, are the sons and the grandsons. And here to-night, on a spot of which the Indian then held long lease, you come to us, another missionary five — only the first fruits, we trust, of these North-western churches, and of this young Seminary. We are here to bid you go. And this council have appointed one who has often spoken to you in the lecture-room, but who will so speak to you no more, to give you their solemn charge.

While I shall not anticipate your particular instructions from the American Board, neither may I forget that we have ordained you specially for the missionary work. Let me then address you with the charge of the great apostle of the Gentiles to his young helper in the work of missions: "Watch thou in all things, endure afflictions, do the work of an evangelist, make full proof of thy ministry."

"Watch" ye; be wakeful and watchful "in all things." And first of all, be watchful over your own hearts. In the delusion that a sacred calling exempts from temptation, you do not share. You know that he who once crawled into Paradise, can linger round the Seminary, can climb the pulpit, or follow on the track of the missionary. You will be encompassed, not alone or chiefly by the ardor of the young convert, but by the low worldliness of the earthen man of China, the gross vices of the out-caste Mahar, by the mummied forms of a dead Christianity. A mission field is not all heaven. Depravity and corruption will be seething around you. Like the sainted Poor, you, too, will get new light on the first chapter of Romans. Now, it was the marvel of Christ's divine humanity that, with a heart day and night in contact with all that was most earthly, that heart beat only of God and heaven. It lay pure as moonlight on a mass of decay. And it is the glory of our missionary band that, from the midst of all that is hard and sensual and hateful, they invariably return to kindle the flame of devotion at home. Such a high spiritual frame, I know, can be maintained only by incessant vigilance. Therefore watch over your hearts with all vigilance, and keep them full of the Holy Ghost.

Be watchful over your lives. I do not warn you against the gravitation of heathen morals, and the poison of the pagan atmosphere all around. I speak of your relations to your missionary brethren. Shut in upon yourselves in fixed relations, specially guard against the friction of a hard and wiry spirit, an unlovely temper, or uncomfortable ways. An uncomfortable man at home, like a live coal, can be hurried along or quietly dropped. *There* he must burn and blister. Even while I am uttering this hint, it seems to me well-nigh superfluous, so wise have commonly been the arrangements of the Board of Missions, and so admirable the spirit of its missionaries. And yet, in view of the infirmities of human nature, and the momentous interests at stake, let me enjoin upon you that heavenly wisdom of practical life which is pure, peaceable, gentle, and easy to be entreated, both toward your missionary brethren and the missionary board.

You must be watchful over your minds. I judge that in all your incessant toils, you shonld not suffer your intellect to rust, nor cease to enlarge your acquisitions. You go to the old homestead of the nations. In spite of his wooden looks, the Chinaman is sharp; the Brahmin is quick and keen at a sophism; and even the Turk can propound to you difficult questions on the Trinity. Your intellectual work will not be all play. Henry Martyn carried with him the highest scholarship of Cambridge, and left behind him the name of the man who never was beaten in an argument. Doubt it not, even in those far-off lands, your power for good will be increased by the whole momentum of your intellectual weight. And often with the sword of the Spirit and the helmet of faith, you will need the spear of Ithuriel too.

Be watchful over the body, as well as the heart and the mind. We send you as laborers, and not martyrs or victims; sacrifices, but living sacrifices. You have spent too many years of preparation to throw away your lives as a thing of naught. Christ's kingdom knows no such economy as that. The Master said: "Occupy till I come." You are to use, and not bury your talent. A late divine once published a sermon entitled "Death a duty." But, brethren, be very sure death is not your duty, so long as you can live to labor. Your sympathies will be sadly, terribly moved by the whiteness of the harvest and the fewness of the reapers. But if you prematurely break yourselves down, you but make the reapers fewer and the harvest sadder. Work, work to the full extent of your powers, but not beyond. Heed the first symptoms of danger, and rescue yourselves for other years of toil. You are too precious an offering to have your heart's blood spilled like water, and every year will add to your value. Remember, at times, the minister who hoped to preach more sermons than Whitefield, but to be longer in doing it. As often, therefore, as you are tempted to destroy yourselves, see that you do it not. But I will tell you what to do. Raise high the signal of distress. Blow long and loud your trumpet to the rescue. Let it echo from the Green Mountains to the Mississippi. Let it reverberate through academy, and college, and seminary, and church. Let it pierce these mothers' hearts; let it stir the young blood in these children's veins; let it disturb the conscience of these sleeping Jonahs and careless Gallios; call louder and louder, till the answer comes. Yea, in all your watching, forget not the church at home. Keep fast hold of the cords ot sympathy. Draw on the prayers and interest of your friends. Help us rouse this young North-west. Hold on upon your fellow students and their successors. Suffer not the missionary line—the noblest of apostolic successions—ever to die out in this your *alma mater.* We charge you in all your watching for souls abroad, watch, also, for missionaries and the missionary spirit at home.

"Endure afflictions" or "hardness." The day is indeed gone by when the missionary was said to take his life in his hands, or even when his departure was thought to be returnless. Fifty years have wrought great changes. But the small number of volunteers proves the work to be still distasteful to flesh and blood. Life-long partings, exile from home and native land—sweet words, young brethren,—loss of society, of culture, of institutions, begin the long catalogue. Then comes the time when you will stand tongue-tied in the face of error and sin, like a motionless soldier before the bayonet charge. There is the long drudgery, the halting speech, perhaps the long, fruitless toils, the bitter disappointment, the half-enlightened convert, and the hypocrite. Families are to be reared in moral Saharas; your comrades droop; the harvest whitens, and beckons, and perishes; the churches are dull of hearing, and the young missionaries slow in coming; a money panic sweeps across the mother-land; a complication of troubles arises at your field of labor, which you can neither cure, nor endure, nor escape. You will indeed reap new joys; but such as these, and many more, will be your afflictions. Endure hardness as good soldiers of Christ. You have served, the most of you, and endured well, as soldiers of your country. One of you helped hold Missouri fast in the Union. One marched to put down conspirators in Indiana. One has been under fire at Memphis and at Corinth, and one of you left his right arm at Vicksburg. Be as willing and as faithful soldiers of the cross as of your country, and we ask no more. [Subdued applause.]

"Do the work of an Evangelist." That, brethren, is your calling. You go to preach the Gospel of repentance and faith to the lost. The anguish, and the search, and the joy of the old man Chu have reached your ears from Tientsin; the call of the dying Chapin has been borne to you from India; you have heard the wail that came from Central Turkey, "begging and imploring" for help.

And now you go to the teeming land where the civilization has come down like a frozen mammoth from the ages past; to that other land, where the first family of the great Aryan race found a home and embalmed itself in a marvelous tongue; and to that other region where Homer sung, and Alexander conquered, and the younger Cyrus began his ill-fated march, where Abram left his father, where Paul was born, and the disciples were first called Christians, and the seven churches had their warnings. But it is not your errand to explore the grotesque civilization of China, to delve in the mine of Sanscrit learning, nor to follow the track of Alexander, or Cyrus, or Abram, or Barnabas and Paul, nor to muse by the ruins of Troy, the banks of the Cydnus, the temple of Diana, or the mud-hovels of the old "Queen of the East." You walk in the footsteps of Christ. You go to pour in the rich light and life of God's love. You go to found other sevens of churches in Asia Minor, to call other men *to be* Christians in Antioch. We do not expect you to shut your eyes and steel your hearts to all the scenes and associations around you, as Howard went through Europe and saw nothing but the inside of its prisons. And yet, in the true meaning of the phrase, you are to know nothing but Christ, and him crucified.

It may be your privilege to add to the mass of obligations with which missions have made science their debtor. Do so if you can. But remember, these things are but the fragrance which religion sheds forth from her vestments, as she walks on her high errand of mercy. Get all the comfort you can, diffuse all the incidental benefits you can, abroad and at home, but evermore do the work of an Evangelist.

And, finally, "make full proof of your ministry." It is the ministry of reconciliation. It rests evermore on those great primal truths — a sin-hating God, a sin-loving world, an atoning Saviour—the only name given under heaven, among men, whereby we must be saved. Remember, we charge you, except as you preach an atoning Saviour, you have no errand to the heathen. They know their sin. They feel God's anger, but they see no hope. The world over, and time through, they have confessed it in penance and sacrifice, in fear and despair. You go to point them to the Lamb of God, that taketh away the sin of the world.

Remember, they are to be sanctified through the truth; and in God's economy the regenerating Spirit follows in the track of the word. Whatever may be our theories as to the possibility that men who know not of Christ, may yet be saved for Christ's sake, if they would but believe in a loving God with a purifying faith; never forget this tremendous and appalling fact, that among the countless millions of our race, the annals of history do not record a dozen cases of such a faith, such a love, and such obedience, except where the word of God has been made known.

Proclaim, then, God's word and not your own speculations. Not merely the milk for babes, but in due time give them the meat for men. Remember you are performing the solemn work of laying the foundations for the far-distant future. Lay them wisely and well. Build on the only foundation, Jesus Christ; build with the gold, silver, and precious stones of divine truth, broad, strong, and high. And, brethren, press home that truth with all its practical, personal power, in the church, in the street, in the house, and by the way. With faith and prayer, urge it home, and then feel, with the noble Judson, that your prospects are "bright." You can trust that truth with the same composure amid the manifold oppositions abroad, as among the infinite scepticisms at home. The living Christ is an ever-living power, and the ministry of Christ a resistless agency. Make but full proof of that ministry, and the end is as sure as the throne and the promise of God.

And now, brethren, go to your work. You are among our jewels, but we lay you on Christ's altar. Would you were more. Sadly but cheerfully we say these parting words. We shall miss your pleasant faces and cheerful voices in our seminary halls. We shall miss you from our festal days, our Alumni gatherings, and convocations of the ministry. We shall miss the warm grasp, and the ever kindly word and look. We shall miss your young enthusiasm and your hearty coöperation in our plans of good for this great North-west. But in Christ's name we bid you go to your distant fields. Only, dear brethren, join hands with us still across the continents; let us feel your warm heart-beat through intervening oceans; from the antipodes let us hear your welcome greeting, and we are content. From the banks of the Ganges, the Yellow Sea, or the old Orontes, and from the shores of Lake Michigan, the paths of duty all converge to the one heavenly home; and there are Woods, and Spring, and Newell, and Judson, with a glorious company and a goodly fellowship, awaiting you and us. Therefore, my dear young brethren, go on your way to the distant nations in the calm and holy confidence of the Master's presence, and in all "the fullness of the blessing of the Gospel of Christ."

PRESENTATION OF THE MISSIONARIES TO THE AMERICAN BOARD.

PROF. J. HAVEN, D.D., CHICAGO THEOLOGICAL SEMINARY.

As the young men who have now been ordained to the ministry of the Gospel, are destined to the special work of Foreign Missions, it seems proper that, in addition to the usual services of ordination, a few words should be spoken more especially consecrating them to that specific work; and so, at their request, in the name, and in behalf of the seminary from which they go forth, and of the churches of the North-west, therein represented, I now present to you, sir, as the representative of the Board, and through you to the cause of missions, these young men, our pupils and our sons.

This Seminary, and the churches which it represents, could give you, sir, no higher proof of their attachment to the American Board, and to the great cause of missions, than the gift which they bring you to-night. For it is not their silver or their gold which they now give you, but that which is dearer and more precious than either — their own sons. And this they do not from their abundance, but of their deep poverty. The value of a gift depends somewhat on the resources of the giver; and whatever, in other respects, may be the resources of the Christian Churches of the North-west, of *men* educated, and fitted for the ministry, they have none to spare. Never was their poverty, in this respect, and their pressing need, greater than now. From the great chain of lakes, on whose border we stand to-night, to the Rocky Mountains, and thence to the far Pacific, hands are outstretched, and voices upraised, saying, *send us men* — men who shall show us the way of salvation, and break unto us the bread of life. Send us those whom you have been educating for the work — those whom we sent to you to be thus instructed. We look upon this field so vast and ready for the harvest, and then upon the little band of Christian students who to-day go forth from our seminary, and say what are these eighteen among so many? Were they multiplied an hundred fold, it would not be enough. And yet from this little band we take out almost one-third the entire number, and set them apart to another destination. We say to our own destitute churches, you can not have all these men. For across the distant ocean other hands are upraised, and other voices are crying out for the bread of life, and in that cry, borne over the seas and mountains of a continent, we recognize the voice of the Master. It comes in at the doors and windows, through the halls of yonder Seminary, and we dare not disregard it. And so to these outstretched Western hands, empty and famishing, we turn and say, touch not the Lord's anointed; touch not those whom the Lord has called to his more distant vineyard; the Master hath need of them. And so, in our poverty, and sad at heart, as we think of our own destitution, yet heartily and joyfully as we look over the field which is the world, we give you these our pupils, our sons, our beloved brethren in Christ, for the work of Foreign Missions.

If ever there was a generous gift, it is this of the churches of the North-west to you to-night. But you have seen something of these Western men, and you know that it is their way to give generously, and to do with all their heart what they do at all. As at the call of their country, they gave generously of their noblest and their best to battle for the true and the right, so now they give of their choicest ones when demanded for Christ and his cause. God's work must not be hindered whatever becomes of us and our little affairs. And so here, O Lord, are we and those whom thou hast given us.

And yet, sir, though we thus speak, I have no fear that we shall be impoverished. These churches, many as they are, and destitute as they are, can well afford to send not these five only, but the whole eighteen if they would go. For is it not the Divine economy that the more we give the more we have ? Has it ever been known in the history of missions, that the Christian Church has grown poor by her generosity, and her devotion to the cause of Christ ? When the poor widow took from the last remaining handful of meal to make a cake for the prophet, it was not diminished, but *multiplied*, by the taking. And so will it be, sir, with these our treasures. We give but to receive again. In the beautiful vision of Ezekiel, the water that flowed out from beneath the temple, at the south of the altar, and flowed on into the desert and into the east country, rapidly widened and deepened as it flowed, and wherever it went, every thing sprang into new life and beauty. So will it be with this little stream that starts forth from our altar to-night on its way to the desert and the east country. It will widen and deepen as it runs. It will become a mighty river. These five young men are but the first fruits — the earnest — the beginning of what this Western land of ours is yet to do for the work of Foreign Missions. There are not less than thirty students, in various stages of the course, in our colleges, who are already committed to this service. The stream is only to the ankles as yet, but a little farther on it is a river that no man can ford, and the desert through which it passes shall burst into verdure, and blossom as the garden of the Lord.

And what shall I say of these young men whom I now present to you. It was a singular Providence that sent to us from our own New England, from our own Massachusetts, your mother and mine, two of her sons, to receive their theological training, wholly or in part, in this Western world, then to pass on to a still more distant field of labor among the heathen. We would not hold them back, much as we value them. They are not ours, but *His*. Of these five, four have been in the service of their country, and go from the field of material conflict to engage in the sterner strife with a spiritual, but not less real or less dangerous foe. They know what suffering and peril are. That empty sleeve testifies of courage and of patriotism. That arm that bore aloft the flag of his country, and held it firm amid the iron hail at the capture of Vicksburg, was left indeed upon the field; but the arm that remains will hold aloft the standard of the Cross on the plains of India, and never suffer it to be lowered or dishonored.

But I must not speak further. It seems but a little time since we welcomed these our young brethren to the Seminary as students. In the few years that they have been with us, we have come to know them and to love them. And now, as they go out from us, they carry with them our sincere esteem, our high appreciation of their intellectual and moral worth, our affection, and our prayers. We shall not forget them. They will not be forgotten by the churches of the North-west. As the mother of Samuel brought the lad to the temple, so to God's altar we come bringing these our sons to-night. We give them to the God of Samuel and of Jacob. We give them to Christ and His Church. And as the mother of Samuel, in the long and solitary hours, wrought for him with her own hands, the little garment, and brought it to him, year by year, as she came to the temple, so for these whom we bring to-night to the altar, willing hands shall toil, and earnest prayers go up, while they are far away among the heathen.

WELCOME AND RIGHT HAND OF FELLOWSHIP.

REV. S. B. TREAT, SECRETARY AMERICAN BOARD.

It is with great satisfaction that I receive these "first-fruits" of your Seminary as the representative of the Board; for them I desire to express my cordial thanks. When, a few months ago, our hearts were so heavily burdened, we little dreamed that the day-spring would appear in the West. We knew that the "star of empire" was passing by us; but we had not learned to say: "Westward the star of *missions* takes its way." During my connection with the Missionary House (twenty-four years), nothing has occurred in our home operations which has so cheered us as this offering of yours. And not us only: word has gone forth to other lands, "Wait a little longer; the West is coming to the rescue."

But I must be allowed to tender my gratulations as well as my thanks. It seems to me that your Seminary has ceased to be a Western institution, and become a national institution, or rather a world-institution. The setting apart of these young men is not done in a corner. It will be talked about and prayed over by *four thousand* churches. The patriarchs of the East will call to mind the ordaining of the *first five* — that event which sent such a quickened life through all our churches, and they will give you their blessing. Mothers in Israel, who have scarcely heard of you till now, will render thanks for "the grace of God bestowed upon" you, and will invoke in your behalf the choicest benedictions.

I know the value of this offering. I know what it will be for us. I know what it would be for the West. I fully believe, however, that your loss will prove to be your gain. By our earthly arithmetic, *five* from *eighteen* leave *thirteen.* But by the celestial arithmetic, subtraction becomes addition. In this instance, I am sure that *five* from *eighteen* will leave, not *thirteen,* nor even *eighteen,* but many more. No. These young men are not lost to the *United States,* but saved rather.

And now, my dear young brethren, with feelings which I can not describe, I turn to you. I am commissioned by the Prudential Committee to tender you the right hand of fellowship. In their name I welcome you to a self-denying but honored service. I welcome you to a partnership with us, in the work of saving the world. I welcome you to the goodly company of the servants of Christ in heathen lands. I welcome you to the joy of beholding Emmanuel's coming glory, as it touches with silver radiance the high places of paganism, and slowly descends to the deeper shadows below. I welcome you to that peace, like a river, which the Great Missionary always keeps in store for such as truly obey his last command. I welcome you to the ineffable smile which, in the final apocalypse, is sure to rest on those who cordially forsake all for Christ.

I have not come here, you perceive, to speak in the "minor mode." No. I regard you as called by the grace of God to the foremost place among the sons of men. I honor the pastorate. To my apprehension there is in the home field no place like it. But you go up still higher. You have entered the Pauline band. With the great apostle you can say, "Unto me who am less than the least of all saints, is this grace given that I should preach among the Gentiles the unsearchable riches of Christ." Would you prove yourselves worthy of your office? Let these words become "as frontlets between your eyes." Rather, let their spirit, as it were the sweetest perfume, pervade the inmost chambers of your being.

In your meditations thereon, be sure to begin where Paul began. "Unto me, who am less than the least of all saints, is this grace given." Lay the foundation of your missionary life in the truest humility. And when you can take your place beside the Apostle in this respect, you will be ready for those other words, "the unsearchable riches of Christ." You will not expect me to dwell upon this theme. I frankly confess that I have not that knowledge of it which I would fain possess. The more I know of the unsearchable riches, the more unsearchable they appear. The more I study them, the more they seem to transcend all study.

Here then we have two of the chief elements of missionary success, I may say of ministerial success—the lowest views of self, and the highest views of Christ. Charles Simeon revealed unconsciously the secret of his great usefulness, when he said: "There are but two objects that for these forty years I have desired to behold;—one is my own vileness; the other is the glory of God in the face of Jesus Christ."

To what we welcome you, you have already heard. There are some things to which we do not welcome you. We do not welcome you to a tempting salary. What we receive ourselves, we give to you—an economical support—nothing more. We do not welcome you to an untroubled and smoothly-flowing life. How much of joy or sorrow may befall you, we must leave in the hands of the Father. We do not welcome you to length of days. We would gladly do it, if we could; but the Angel of Death is obedient to another will than ours. We do not welcome you to great visible success. If you live to three score years, or three score and ten, you will see important changes, I doubt not; some, perhaps, that you do not anticipate. That noble missionary who has just gone up to his heavenly home (Dr. Goodell) sailed into the Golden Horn in the early summer of 1831. He found himself in a city fitted by its position to be the queen of the earth. But, alas! what intense bigotry did he find! What bitter hatred of the truth! A death penalty, sure to be enforced, hung above the head of every Moslem. "Renounce Islam and die," was the brief formula. He, and those who joined him, toiled on four and twenty years, guiding inquirers to Christ, and gathering churches; when, lo! that which they had not dared to hope for at first, came to pass. That old death penalty was swept away! How? "War did it," says one. "Diplomacy did it," says another. But neither could have done it—both together could not have done it, *without the Missionary*. "The poor wise man saved the city."

At times you may grieve for your poor success, just as pastors do at home. You may bewail, for instance, the shortcomings of your converts. But when the burden is heavy upon you, read Paul's epistles. And remember, especially, that God seeth not as man seeth. Ten years ago, it was the lamentation of missionaries in all parts of India, that their churches had so little of Christian manliness. Just then, however, the Sepoy rebellion burst upon the world. And when the storm had passed by, it was found that these feeble, sickly children of theirs had met the shock with a courage and firmness that became their wonder and delight.

No. We do not welcome you to assured success, but to just so much as the Master shall be pleased to give you, commending his own words to your prayerful study, "According to your faith be it unto you." And there will be single scenes in your history, I doubt not, which will amply repay you for all your toil; as when a missionary of ours stood by a dying Hindoo, and heard him say, feebly, faintly, "Christ has taken all of mine, and given me all of his." "Ah! what has he taken of yours?" "Sin, Sir; death, Sir." "What has he given you of his?" "Heaven, Sir; holiness, Sir."

But I must crave the privilege of saying a few words to these pastors, and these Christian friends. These young men, as you see, are going down to the dark, cold shadows of heathenism. As Carey expressed it, they are *going down into the well*. Will *you* hold on to the ropes? They are entering upon a life-campaign; will you equip them, as you did those regiments which fought so bravely for the stars and stripes, and afterward furnish food and raiment? To put the matter in a definite shape, will you advance your contributions twenty per cent.? I believe you will do it. I do not see how you can help it. Rather, I think you will rejoice in the opportunity.

But I have something more to say. For the last nine months I have felt a weight upon my spirit almost too heavy to be borne. I have asked myself, Oh how many times! "When is the world to be given to Christ? He whose right it is, the Prince of the Kings of the earth, when is He to be enthroned in all the world?"

I have no distrust of present methods. It was after that bloody death, and under the opening heavens, that the command was given, "Preach the gospel to every creature." We are on the right track, therefore; but how slow the train moves! Four thousand churches represented by one hundred and forty ordained missionaries in all the heathen world!

The heathen world! Do we think what this is? Let us suppose it to pass before us—say ten abreast—a living, slow-moving current. From morning to night, from night to morning, the ear is burdened by its heavy, incessant tread. At the pace of one mile an hour, it would consume six years in passing by us, a long, unresting funeral train! At first we are awe-struck and speechless. Myriads upon myriads, millions upon millions; and all traveling, like ourselves, to the judgment seat, and almost all ignorant of the way of life!

Suppose, now, that we should resolve at once to enter, with our whole hearts, upon the work of the world's reconstruction. How appalling would the endeavor seem!

But hopeless as is the undertaking, on the human side, on the divine side, it is perfectly feasible. See what marvels the Providence of God has wrought for missions. A little more than *twenty* years ago, and China was shut against the Christian world — locked, bolted, barred. But we have been told quite recently, that it is now open in all its length and breadth.

With what skill and patience has He exalted the valleys and made low the mountains and hills of Hindoostan. First, papal France was to be excluded from the land, as having no lot or inheritance there. Next the power of the native princes, idolatrous, oppressive and effete, was to be cast down; and then a vast trading company, selfish as the love of pounds, shillings and pence could make it, was to be led along by a hook in the nose, till the set time should come for saying, "Pass on; *your* work is done." And now one of the noblest of Christian men holds the vice regal sceptre over nearly *two hundred millions* of Hindoos.

And look at Madagascar. When the missionaries were expelled thirty years ago, they left a few disciples, without a ministry, with no right to meet for worship, no right to read a book, hated, hunted, in constant danger of a cruel death. But they also left two injunctions, to wit: "Cleave to the Bible, and cleave to one another;" and they did so. They came together, in fear and trembling, and read the Scriptures. After a time it was discovered that some had more skill than others in explaining "the lively oracles;" and they were asked to take upon themselves the ministry of the word. But there were no sacraments. How, for instance, should these persecuted ones commemorate the death of Christ? What else to do, they knew not, and so they asked their teachers to perform this service. When, therefore, Mr. Ellis went there in 1861, he found that a native ministry had sprung up, in spite of all repressing influences, having received its anointing, not from bishops, or presbyters, or councils, but from the Holy Ghost; and the Lord has blessed those servants of His, as also the missionaries who have gone there since, so that the number of communicants is ten times greater than it was in 1861.

What now is the world's chief need? A single word contains the answer. FAITH. *A believing Church might see the speedy triumph of Christ, in all the earth.* Know ye not, my brethren, that God has placed the entire resources of his kingdom at our disposal? Elisha was wroth with the King of Israel because he struck the ground but thrice. "Thou shouldst have smitten five or six times," he said; "then hadst thou smitten Syria till thou hadst consumed it. And that scene by the Mount of transfiguration! "Master, I have brought unto thee my son, which hath a dumb spirit." And then having told his story of suffering and trial, he said: "If thou canst do any thing, have compassion on us and help us." Jesus said unto him, "If thou canst believe, all things are possible to him that believeth."

Were there time, I would gladly say a few words as to *what* we should believe. But I will only glance at two particulars: First, We should believe that *Christ is waiting to see of the travail of his soul, and be satisfied.* He that died for this very end—he is waiting for the tardy movements of his Church. Second, We should believe that *there is soul-travail for us as well as for him.* As by reason of his human nature, he can be touched with a feeling of our infirmities, so we are to share his sorrows and his joys. Remember how he wept over Jerusalem, looking down from Olivet, and then think what it must be for him to look down upon a world lying in wickedness, beholding all the crimes which are committed, thoughts that can not bear the light of the sun, and then glancing through all the ages of the future, knowing perfectly what a lost spirit may become, what a lost spirit must suffer.

It remains for me to give you the right hand of fellowship in behalf of the council. In the name of these pastors and delegates, in the name of the Churches which have sent them hither, as also of all the Churches of the North-west represented in some sort by them, I give you this right hand. It is not a vain ceremony. I have learned that no men have so wide a place, in so many hearts, as those who go to the heathen. In times of trial call this scene to mind, and take comfort and courage therefrom.

A few years ago, a party of missionaries was about to leave Persia for America. They were to travel under a hot sun, over bridgeless rivers, along rough and precipitous ways, pitching their tents in insecure places, till they should take a steamer at Trebizond, and afterward to take a sailing vessel to Smyrna. A Nestorian girl, just as they were setting forth, made a prayer, so simple, so scriptural, and so appropriate to your circumstances, that I will ask the congregation to join me in offering it for you, only changing two or three words in the last sentence: "Dear Father! let not the sun smite them by day, nor the moon by night. Give thine angels charge concerning them, to bear them up in their hands, that they dash not a foot against a stone. When they pass through the deep rivers, let not the waters overflow them. Let the Angel of the Lord encamp round about their moving tabernacle. Spread a table for them in all the long wilderness. When they come to the fire-ship, let not the flames kindle upon them. When they come to the winged vessel, though the waves go up to heaven and down to hell, keep them in the hollow of thy hand, and bear them safely to the desired haven. Let not their dust mingle with the dust of father or the dust of mother; but let it mingle with the dust of their children, with them to hear the last trump, with them to meet the Lord in the air, to be forever with him, all safely home!"

www.ingramcontent.com/pod-product-compliance
Lightning Source LLC
LaVergne TN
LVHW020635110826
845149LV00004B/1199
9781418191542